PASSAGE OUT OF TIME

POEMS ABOUT TIME, AGE, LIFE AND DEATH

BY

JOAN JUTTNER, M.D.

Published by

Two Worlds Publishing

P.O. Box 700409
Oostburg, Wisconsin 53070

Copyright by Joan Juttner
All rights reserved

Printed in United States of America
For permission to reprint poems in this
volume contact the publisher
at the above address

Cover Photograph by Mark C. Hopkins

ISBN-13: 978-0-9830957-0-5
ISBN-10: 0-9830957-0-1

Dedicated To

Udo

And In Memoriam To

Perry

Thank You to Gina Garrett
for Editorial Assistance

Thank You to Hans U. Juttner
for Proofreading

PASSAGE OUT OF TIME

Table of Contents

Thief 1
Passage Out Of Time 2
Time 3
Gift Of Time 4
On JFK's Death 5
Rosetta's Man 6
When You Leave 9
Worth the Try 11
To Live 12
Tomorrow 13
The Tired Day 14
Midafternoon 15
Wooden Soldiers 16
Saving the Past 17
Nature Of Our Interlude 18
Two Civilizations 19
For Most 20
Rebirth 21
Eons 22
Thread Of Life 23
My Brother On 9/11 24
Hydrogen Bombs and Hybridomas 25
Stop Death 26
Doctor's Prayer 27
The Furthest Field 28
With the Coming Of the New Year 29
The Autopsy 33
Killing Time 34
Full Circle 35
Dear President Reagan 36
Tears 37
Old Rag Mountain 38
His Master's Gone 43

Your Father's Gone 44
The Caller Wore Black 45
The Funeral 47
Perry's Eulogy 48
Earth's Cemetery 49
Turn Left At Albuquerque 50

THIEF

Oh, Time,
Justice will not
Prosecute you though you
Steal from us the days and nights of
Our lives.

Ω

PASSAGE OUT OF TIME

The moment we go through the birth canal
And pass into time,
We are programmed for the earthly end.

Our cells carry the concealed codes
That determine who we are
And the timer which will turn off the switch.

Our souls carry forth the canons
That reveal why we are
And empower our passage out of time.

Ω

TIME

Time stops for no man,
Not even for God.
Age follows with the years,
As plants leave the sod.

A sage marks the passing years
By the wisdom gained.
A fool watches years escape
Till few or none remain.

Tomorrow and tomorrow are
Until they are no more;
And caught looking backwards
Comes a closed door.

But today is here and assured,
And all of it is real.
So live in it and love in it,
And know what you feel.

Age overtakes the man
Who dallies on the way;
But years seem not to pass
In the fervor of today.

You must enjoy the years;
They come and go no more.
Each age of man is the best
That God gives us to explore.

Ω

GIFT OF TIME

If I could give you time,
Plucked from a physicist's equation,
Drawn out from all the forces
That have moved it since creation,

Would you celebrate this gift?
What would you do with infinity?
Could you belong to endlessness?
Could you be happy, ever fifty?

"Enough of this!" you would say,
"How boring, let's get on with it.
Unless, perhaps, you could find a way
Where we all could benefit."

For I would give you eons,
Untouched by ferment of stagnation,
And wisdom nurtured by experience,
For time is the clock of appreciation.

Ω

ON JFK'S DEATH

The days go by and I can see
That my tomorrows may not be.

A young man dies, and his young son
Does not know that he is gone.

With promise spent in time so short,
Promise that some bullets thwart,

I fear that time which I ignore
May all too soon shut my door.

Time will not fill the pen I use,
Nor make my brain the less obtuse;

So I must write, if write I must
Of things that history will not dust.

Ω

ROSETTA'S MAN

Winter was as hard as the ice it made.
Snow fell, rising to the top of the barn door;
Never thawing, it drifted into spring.
The sky turned liquid gray.
Rains drowned the sodden earth
That tried to hold the melting snow.
Nature never knows what's enough.
The banks of the April creek burst
Till it became a river and then a lake,
Swirling a sordid collection of silt and seeds
Over the bottom land.

Rosetta's man lived on the high ground.
His farm was chiseled out of
Rocky impotent bluffs above the creek.
The kind of place you work harder on
And get less from.
He and Rosetta had poor man's money,
Six children.
They come in handy
When you have to fight and beat the earth.
But Rosetta's man didn't have to worry--
The flood was far below him.

The neighbor did.
He owned the bottom ground,
Rich land...so he was richer.

His black velvet loam suckled seeds
Into a prairie jungle

That always topped the county yield.
His corn climbed
Till the tassels tickled the sky,
Then burst forth with fat, full-kernelled ears
That laughed back at the sun
With a wide-toothed grin.

But this year, the creek turned on this man
Who lived well off the soil it nurtured.
It raged and demanded a toll:
It wanted his cattle.

Rosetta's man got on his horse, rode down
To help the neighbor save his herd.

The flood was a wild woman,
Throwing rubble like plates,
Hurrying in hostile pursuit
Of everything and nothing,
Up this gully, down that ditch,
Here, there, everywhere,
Madly searching for the way out
To the Mississippi.

The current boiled, logs torpedoed,
And the horse shied.
He lost his footing
On ground he knew when it was dry,
Throwing Rosetta's man;
In panic he heaved and his hoof hit the head
Of the man who fed him, loved him,
Whom he loved.

The neighbor was nearby,
But not close enough.

He dragged his friend from the torrent,
And sacrificed his cows to God.
But it did no good;
Rosetta's man was dead.

The sun came to the funeral,
Smiling hesitantly between the clouds,
As if to apologize that it wasn't there
When it was needed.
Then the days passed again into the ordinary.

Spring brought Rosetta fifteen years
Of coaxing the land
To produce proud poverty,
Of raising kids
Beyond rocky hard mere existence.
The neighbor did what he could to help her.
But there's a limit to what can be offered,
And still more to what can be accepted.

Ω

WHEN YOU LEAVE

Go in springtime
When new grass blades bend under foot
And mend as young hearts do.

Go with the blossoms
As they fade to seed that I may plant again
And nourish what is left of me.

Go in summer's sun
When the earth is bleached as raw and dry
As my eyes are.

Go after sundown
When night shadows shroud your likeness
Into the eternal trees.

Go in autumn
When dead leaves break beneath your feet
And in my seasoned heart.

Go with rising winds
When they bring storms that thrash the earth
And match my turmoil.

Go in winter
When snow whitens my hair with wisdom
That I may understand.

Go in death
When your aged bones walk through infinity.
I will miss you more, not less.

But, do not go!
I do not want to know you have gone;
I <u>cannot</u> say good-bye.

Ω

WORTH THE TRY

Where are we going and what will we do?
And will it matter when we are through?

Should we not ramble along the way?
And see the joy there is in a day?

Should we not see the trials that come
As something that happens to everyone?

Should we not think that life is to live,
For the <u>inner</u> pleasure that it can give?

And then we can say, on coming to die,
That all that we did was worth the try.

Ω

TO LIVE

We must walk the varied fields on this earth;
Know a life beyond the borders of our birth,

Collect like gold the dust on butterfly wings;
Love the soft shadows where our heart sings,

Seek refuge with the birds in a cozy ark;
Hear laughter when bound by a dismal dark,

Bathe in the warmth of each others tears,
That we know grace in the remaining years.

Ω

TOMORROW

Does tomorrow come? When we're not tired,
And dreams are born, we've so long sired.

When the sun gives heat till the soul is fired,
And our limp lives are again inspired.

When we will have time for us to do
The undone things we've wanted to.

To read the words and play the song,
And never think: will it take too long?

To sow seeds and watch plants grow.
Or put ink in a pen and let words flow.

Or just do nothing but sit and think,
In a day that's ours and does not shrink.

Gone is fatigue that clouds the mind,
And keeps our goals so far behind.

Does tomorrow come? It's an unreal thing.
And we really don't know what it will bring.

Today may go, taking our bodies with it.
Or, worse than that, it may take our spirit.

Ω

THE TIRED DAY

The tired day sweats
And stains the sky orange,
Hurries westward toward the earth's rim,
Heaves heavy clouds along its path,
Crawls from the city, stumbling into twilight,
Weary from the warring winds.

The tired day moves into a black knit forest,
Pauses, drinks of gentle silence,
And catalyzed by the cadence of the crickets,
Moored in peace, rekindling begun,
Creeps between the covers of the night.

Ω

MIDAFTERNOON

From the hesitant hue of birthing of today
And the peeping penumbra
Of apprentice talents,
The sun ripens by noon.

By midafternoon she is in command,
On duty, sharp and hot,
The unrelenting inventor.
With sinewy vigor and a silent tune,
She yields a salty sweat in casks.
With a Machiavellian artistry
From the heat of her furnace,
Magnifying the full-colored kaleidoscope
Of nature, she works with a
Self-indulgent narcissism of productivity,
And becomes a proverb,
A fecund spawning genesis.

No hint of a slide into a burnished dusk,
No bored endings, no echoes, no half-lives,
Midafternoon is the peak,
The here and now,
But not the forever.

Ω

WOODEN SOLDIERS

The years are wooden soldiers
Who always win their war,
Unbending and unyielding,
Marching on forever more.

But they can be defeated,
Ignored, as in child's play,
By sitting them aside
For the beauty of each day.

Ω

SAVING THE PAST

We rummage through the dust of our lives,
The scenes of joy and sorrow we have saved.
Time and daily living soften images,
Like light fades a photograph to muted tones.

We have boxed many thousand memories
And hid them in our attic,
Saved like a rare old wine—never drunk,
Shreds of us, tiny gems in an antique broach,
Treasured but never worn, all but forgotten.
Too precious for the day to day.

Should we sell our antiques?
Trade them for abstract art,
Fast cars and jugs of cheap wine?
Or dust them off to evolve again?

Ω

NATURE OF OUR INTERLUDE

A forest overgrown with honeysuckle;
Rootless trees fallen to a greater good.
These essentials of a bird sanctuary
Are our wild and wonderful wood.

Family, friends, a bit of reverie,
A job well done, laughter, and solitude,
All become the garden of our souls,
And define the nature of our interlude.

Ω

TWO CIVILIZATIONS

Two civilizations spoke
Of the unknown,
Of the gift of life,
Of their ignorance.

With no knowledge of each other,
They dreamed,
They created,
They worshiped.

Time eclipsed their existence
To ruins,
To chance,
To diggings.

Today we admire in awe
Their similarities,
Their searching,
Their inspirations.

Knowing that we are like them,
Still puzzled,
Still planning,
Still reverent.

Ω

FOR MOST

Life is always spent
In a waiting room, and yet
Most of us assume....

Ω

REBIRTH

A birthday is not an anniversary,
But, instead, a day of rebirth.
A day to undertake a thoughtful query
Of our quest upon this earth.
A day to cast off a ragged memory
By now grown used and secondhand.
A day to hear the echo of eternity
And hope to understand.
A day to find the fingers of creativity
In the glove of God's hand.
A day to take on a fresh relativity,
Made from the dust of earth.
A day to take clay and capability,
And mold from them fresh rebirth.

Ω

EONS

Somewhere in the hollows of our repertoires
Ageless genes hanker after eons.
We marched to the drum on 'fours',
Until the sacrospinal and the psoas tightened
And fixed our gaze directly on the horizon.
We wrote on rocks, hieroglyphs remain,
Though Nature has recombined our genes.
We have seen the finite come and go,
Our link to forever: words written yesterday,
And the promise of our God for tomorrow.

Ω

THREAD OF LIFE

Aborigines today, who live in the past,
Spin a thread of life spanning ages so vast

That eons stopped and moments were gone;
Yet the core of existence bravely moved on;

Because all was there that mankind requires,
The food, the shelter, the warmth of fires.

Yet man's intellect marches to a luring peak,
Ignoring atoms, and inheritance by the meek.

Ω

MY BROTHER ON 9/11

He called on his cell phone talking of danger.
His building was on fire, filled with smoke.

He was wearing black, white, olive skin.
He was like so many; he knew what is right.

He cared for people; he laughed with his kids.
He did his work, had several jobs:

Stockbroker, janitor, fireman, accountant;
Provider, spouse, friend, parent, rescuer...

He celebrated God on a his own day or hour.
He lived by rules of goodness that govern us.

I am putting his picture here, by the others.
If you see him, call me at 21 2-MANY NOS.
      (numbers).

Ω

HYDROGEN BOMBS AND HYBRIDOMAS

The newspaper speaks of hydrogen bombs
and hybridomas.

This is a ragged end of a day,
Empty as holes in socks needing mending,
Torn into so many scraps of things to be done
It wouldn't even make a crazy quilt.

The newspaper speaks of hydrogen bombs
and hybridomas.

Life is paid for in supermarkets,
Told by alarm clocks,
Cooked into soup for supper,
And tucked under a pillow like a baby tooth.

The newspaper speaks of hydrogen bombs
and hybridomas.

I can make orange marmalade.
Is it not, after all, profound?
If it sets well,
It won't run off the bread,
Will be enjoyed and then--be gone.

The newspaper speaks of hydrogen bombs
and hybridomas.

Ω

STOP DEATH

We are taught
How to treat
And save lives;
But not
How to stop Death.

Ω

DOCTOR'S PRAYER

Poor wrinkled bag of bones, only living
Until you can manage to be gone;
Fighting with a stinking, rotten tumor
To maintain <u>any</u> kind of liaison.
We watch as the rest of you decays,
Gobbled up by a mob of hungry cells,
That has no sense of symbiosis,
And guts the home in which it dwells.

We have no license to give further help;
Only God can provide relief.
We can offer up a prayer for speed,
To take a life worse than death's grief.

Ω

THE FURTHEST FIELD

Stand a far field from the patient.
Measure his words as symptoms,
Read his aura in the data
From the lab and X-ray images,
And know his illness,
But never know him.

A disease can be a death sentence;
And the victim's past, filled with
Fashion pages and finery
Or board rooms and dollars,
Fades into meaningless vignettes.
Reality carries no jokes.

The truth is what is coming,
And the pathologist acts as
The notary affixing a short future,
Sure as night, falling leaves, burnt coals,
And such bleak endings
Tear the pronouncer's soul.

For the patient creeps
Inside the microscope,
And appears, along with his diagnosis,
In visions, sharp as a scalpel,
To cut the physician
Who gets too close.

Ω

WITH THE COMING OF THE NEW YEAR

I bundled my feelings in a wrapper
I hoped would not tear and dialed her
number. Over the phone I could hear the
dismay displayed on her face as clearly as if
she had been sitting across a kitchen table
from me.

"My sister thought she had gallbladder
trouble. She's 42. But they did an
ultrasound and it was o.k."
She drew a breath, with a sigh that said more
than the facts and continued, "So then they
did an upper GI and found gastro-esophageal
reflux and told her that would explain her
discomfort. But she's a nurse and she
thought it must be more than that. So then
they did a chest X-ray and found the tumor,
in the right lung. And next they did a bone
scan and it has gone to her lumbar spine,
and her sternum is almost gone, just little
bits left. And now the CAT scan shows
nodules scattered through the liver. They did
a biopsy and it is adenocarcinoma."

With the weight of her words and the quick
catches of breath between, I knew she did not
fool herself with the hope that all would go
away. "What questions should we ask the
oncologist; maybe you, being a physician, can
help us with what we should ask."

In this moment which expected miracles, I could not deliver. But I could find some small salvage to begin to bring her to the point she was already at, to this silent secret she knew...yet could not say.

So I offered what little expertise I could for this sad story, "There are different kinds of adenocarcinoma. Some grow very slowly. You could ask him what he thinks the prognosis might be. How long ..."

"Oh, we did and he said he wouldn't touch that question. What do you think?" She was searching for an answer as impossible as the sun at night. Yet she knew -- her tone told the truth, but her words circled reality.

I spun my thoughts to threads that she might weave to wisdom. "Well, it would seem to me that if it were the slow growing type, he might have said so, but since he didn't, that suggests to me that it is not a friendly kind. And since it is already in the liver and bones...," I had eased in the awful ugliness as easily as I could.

She was ready for it, "It's not good, is it?" Her words fell under the weight of their message. "But they are going to give her radiation. Would they do that if they didn't think they could treat it?"

"It depends. It can ease discomfort." I said.

"She is having a lot of pain, in her sternum-- it's very bad. This has all happened in the last two weeks, since Christmas." She enunciated the word with the portent of a catastrophe.

"Radiation therapy will shrink the tumor. They want to scar it down and that very often relieves the pain. But, you see, it is in a lot of places so to radiate would be hard." I could not say, as impossible as the sun rising in the west.

She only needed my ears, for in my listening she found strength, "We worry about my parents. They are in their seventies; I don't know how they will take it. She is my middle sister. I'm the youngest. We have an older sister, and our brother is the oldest. She was always their favorite. Just by a tiny bit."

She paused to swallow the poison of her faults. "I wonder if it is some sort of payment for her place in my parents feelings. And then I wish it could be me because they would not be hurt quite so much."

Her emotions were as familiar as the noonday sun, always there, scorching the wounds of what does not go away.

She prevailed over her pain to say, "This is neither here nor there, but my brother, he's the oldest. He was a priest, but he left the order. He wouldn't come for Christmas unless his, what would you call him, his partner could come."

"Did he come?" This answer would determine how the sun would set on this sad story.

"My mother phoned me up to ask me what I thought, what about my kids. I told her it would not be a problem for my family. But they should decide. It is their home, they are his parents. And so he came, with his friend. They chose to keep him, to try to understand him."

She paused in realization. She explained things to herself as much as to me. "We're a close, ethnic family. "My parents come from Yugoslavia. They are the Old World. My mother, she's so gentle, soft. The housewife who leans on her husband. My father has that, I don't know another word, maleness. So stoic. In charge. When something was broken, he would fix it. He could fix anything. But he can't fix my sister."

Her voice quivered with the vibrato of sequestered tears. "Together we will see it through."

Ω

THE AUTOPSY

You did not say that much to me,
Old scarred heart,
That finally skipped one beat too many.

I searched for why you lived,
Instead of why you died,
For variance, pathology, uniqueness.

But you were like all of us,
No humors in your spleen,
No seat of mirth or melancholy.

In your gut you hid
The pervasive endings
Of daily consumption and controversy.

Your airless lungs once breathed
The silent whispers we all know
And never tell one each other.

Like all of us, you lived and died in solitude,
With suffocated synapses
Unable to truly touch those around you.

Your secrets have gone with you,
Hidden in patterned gyri,
Never unraveled, though I tried.

Ω

KILLING TIME

Try to kill Time.
Her lungs are crepitant.
Ever swollen with a fleeting breath.

She is quick and sure,
A pulsing drummer of infinity,
But as heartless as a metronome.

Try to dissect her,
That wombless woman
Filled with nulliparous appointments.

Her gut stretches beyond the universe,
A warehouse of digested fragile moments.
Gone forever to waste.

She eludes the autopsy surgeon.
But he, like all of us,
Knows her hollow insides.

Would she were dead and we ageless.

Ω

FULL CIRCLE

What begins as an infant, ends as an infant.
Sure hands that led the second generation
Palsy, leaving scratches on the sands of time.
Tongues that, seemingly a fortnight ago
Issued wise rhetoric, thicken,
Yielding a jam of nonsense.
Skin, weathered by wisdom,
Thins to baby tenderness and breaks down.
Weighted brains shrink
To wide furrows and narrow ridges and
Ventricles like lakes where faculties drown;
Reason withers as caulk-clogged channels
Choke off life's last, last, last drops of blood;
Knotted neurons short-circuit today.
Eyes that used to speak by themselves
Are wordless, vacant and confused;
Their *arcus senilis* tunnel vision to the past,
To see daughters making mud pies with eggs,
Herself sewing feed sack dresses for school.
The retracing feet weaken, shuffling,
Tottering, stumbling, falling into bed.
God waits with a basket to pick up
The old bones shattered by society's pace.
Old winter wind blows across
The wasteland of minds that taught all
And forgot all,
And rattles the last exit door.

Ω

DEAR PRESIDENT REAGAN

My mother would have cast her vote for you,
But she could not know you were running.
What meaning meant she no longer knew.
Her brain had lost its cunning.

She really did know you, long years ago,
Since her little tykes, my sister and I,
Sang on the Barn Dance over WHO.
You, their Communicator that time verified.

"I wish he'd run; he'd be good." She'd said,
Before her mind slipped into a dry bog.
While our nation, our world was being led
By you, who now lives in your own dense fog.

She was sightless, soundless, ever remote
You were President without her proud vote.

Ω

TEARS

Tears,
Flow freely,
Dampen the drought of the soul
In sorrow.

Ω

OLD RAG MOUNTAIN

A long haired shepherd dog approached us.
His bright orange jacket said 'Rescue'.
Behind him came a forest ranger
And a young man and woman.

"Were you here over Labor Day weekend?"
"No, why do you ask?" I wondered.
"We are looking for someone. He was last
Seen then, here on the mountain."
"What does he look like?" I asked.

How stupid a question;
Labor Day was two weeks ago.
"I have a picture," the park ranger said,
Pulling a crumpled paper from her pocket.

An over-blackened copier image.
Early twenties. Naval academy uniform.
Flag behind him. All-American. Very fit.
His formal smile announced that
He had arrived into the adult world
Confident, a continuation of a valued species.

"I smelled something dead, coming up here."
My husband sensed my advancing thoughts.
"Enough said." He cautioned.
My profession marched to the front of my
mind. "I'm a pathologist.
You are dealing with smells, a week or so."

So it was out, death, the blunt truth,
Hard as the rocks under foot.
The ranger slowed my thoughts,
"Assuming he is dead."

The young woman's face flickered.
Was it fear or faith I saw forced from her?
Was the cadet her friend, her lover,
Perhaps the future father of her children?
What right had I to kill the last kernel left of him?

The young man moved closer to me,
As if I knew something, clairvoyantly.
"Would a human smell the same as an animal?" He asked.
"Yes," I answered, with all the audacious authority of an addle brain,
"My first autopsy was on a floater.
He was a caught for a month under water..."
Then reason rushed in, if much too slowly.

But, by now, the ranger wished to ask
My professional opinion,
"But Labor Day was two weeks ago.
Would there still be a smell?"

"It has been cold. That slows decomposition;
And he may not have died two weeks ago,"
I suggested.

She considered this and agreed, "Yes,
He might have been alive until last week
When Hurricane Fran came through."

Where did you notice the smell?"

I tried to think. My first time here.
"Was it after the streams?" She prompted.

"Yes, after that, but I didn't notice where.
I thought a squirrel had died or something."

"Before the fire road narrows to a path?"

"Yes, I think it was along
Where all the big trees have blown down,
Except the one dead snag right in the middle,
As if some strange wind,
Tornado-like, had come through."

"I know where you mean, a lot of debris and
damage from Hurricane Fran." She said.

I paused. The cadet took on a life and
The panic of his parents overtook me.
Where was their cherished child,
Their prized treasure
Who possessed their feelings?
Where was their trophy to all,
Their semblance of self,
Their issue who carried their inscriptions,
Their embodiment of expectation,
Their fulfillment of the future of forever?

The ranger brought me back,
"We have him for picking up scents."
She pointed to the shepherd.
They pushed on.

"I said too much, didn't I?"
Was he just a clinical object to me?
Did those hollow haunts of retirement
Make me eager to use my unused knowledge,
To turn the story into mine?

What about him;
Why had he come to the mountain?
Could he have been searching
For why he lived?
Did he find answers to affronts here?
Was he at home among the roots of Nature?

We trekked upwards;
Alert to the endurance of evermore,
To green acorns and fallen leaves,
To tinged blooms and scattered seeds;
Aware of the forecast of nevermore
Of the autumn of the end.

Stretched out on smooth bedrock
On top of the mountain,
The sun and the smiles of my husband
Warmed my chilled spirit and searching soul.
The value of the cadet, of me,
Of our lives was intertwined.
I knew whose story this was:
His, mine, yours, everyone's,
The story we all face and never face.

When passersby worship this wilderness,
They pass his pine bough casket
And bid an unknown good-bye.
The wind plays his funeral dirge;
The trees shelter the shells of his bones;
The boulders are his tombstone,
Their crevices his crypt;
The wildflowers carpet his grave;
The birds sing hymns of passage.
For he is here, on Old Rag Mountain.

Ω

HIS MASTER'S GONE

For days, no months, back and forth he went,
Between the house, the barn, and the road.
The dog could not know of the accident,
So he kept on searching, never slowed.

Where could he be--gone so long?
The question stayed on Snowball's face.
He kept up his vigil, ever strong;
No one could take his master's place.

Round the barn; cock a look at the truck;
Stand wagging his tail by the kitchen door;
Trot up the road---with a little luck...
He could not know he would come no more.

With envy I asked, as I learned to cope;
Was it not better to live with some hope?

Ω

YOUR FATHER'S GONE

On this day, when memory arches
To become a circle,
Your father visits your visions,
He whom you knew too short a time.
He was with you, a guide
To your enthusiasm, so fertile,
As you, the child, the son, almost grown,
Prepared to break the girdle
Of passage, sure that life ahead would
Provide an ending rhyme.

Then he was gone forever,
In wild days of coma and collapse,
He who knew there were answers,
And questions, a right and wrong,
He whose counsel held forth
Directions to mazes and from maps,
He who left untold the subtle signals
To which an adult adapts.
And you, ever bewildered,
Have searched for him
Your whole life long.

Ω

THE CALLER WORE BLACK

Her guests were scolded for wearing black.
No matter she was ninety,
They were not death calling.
Her tongue lashed out
And wounded their intent,
Their friendliness, them.

Fear stalked the house at night.
Sometimes it would turn on the back lights.
Sometimes it would climb the porch steps.
Sometimes it would peek into the window.

Come morning there would be no trace.
The aging children shook their heads,
Turned their eyes from the moments of truth,
And agreed, with lies,
To what had not happened.

She tottered, feebly, from the table,
Undernourished, empty but never hungry,
Except for the conversation at dinner
With those who were not there to answer.

The food molded along with her.
It sat uneaten, over-ripe like her.
Something that should have been tossed out
But instead was forgotten, then rotten.

Cataracts hid the disarray and dust
And the telltale story of time passing--
The fading fabric of the furnishings,
The cracked frame around the oil painting.

Between naps and night she sorted
Her memories: blurred photos, old letters,
The snippet cut from a yellowed newspaper,
The saying handwritten on a tattered scrap.

Weakness from her paltry meals
And the endless years of aging
Brought her down, with vivid pain.
One leg, underpinning of her life, cracked.
Death called, wearing black,
Rattling the back door.

$$\Omega$$

THE FUNERAL

The songbird sang for the last good-bye.
The wind stirred a chill as angels flew by.
There is no answer to the question why.

The sleet stung sharp as a mourner's sigh.
The cold brought ice to each tear-filled eye.
There is no answer to the question why.

The daffodils waved the last good-bye.
Her garden ended as she came to die.
There is no answer to the question why.

The angel wings whipped the winds to cry.
From the day of birth we must reckon to die.
There is no answer to the question why.

She passed through the clouds that
Curtained the sky.
And all of us pondered why we live and die.
But there is no answer to the question why.

Ω

PERRY'S EULOGY

We want you here, smiling and laughing;
Your eyes dancing with joy at Lynn, the kids.
We want you here petting your cats.
Reminiscing with your brothers and mom
About growing up on the farm in Iowa.
Hanging out with us,
Sharing supper and stories;
Going to Chargers games and Disneyland;
Taking us through the backlot at Universal;
Leading your team
For the Fire, Search and Rescue group;
Attending movies; hosting game nights;
Voting on Survivor.
We want you here
For all the movies you could have made;
To follow your leadership shooting films;
To see your scripts made into
Blockbusters for the big screen;
To inspire fellow writers with your ideas;
To share in your future successes
As we did with the past ones:
Eagle Scouts, screenwriting, films.
Instead we celebrate your life,
Your family and multitude of friends,
Realizing the world is a better place
Because you lived.
Part of you will live on
Through all of us whom you touched.
We hope to see your name in the titles
As screenwriter of a movie.
But for now, glowing bright as the sun,
Your star is born in heaven.

Ω

THE EARTH'S CEMETERY

The earth's cemetery was
Shrouded in drab gray,
A pocked moonscape,
Of shifting sand, shiftless lizards,
Free-aiming sagebrush, no abiding roots.

Nature had the wind help
Earth build a few monuments
To break the monotony:
Broken toothed mountains,
Kaleidoscope canyons,
And tombstone rocks that outlived
The men who wrote upon them.

God watches over graveyards.
But He was disappointed
In this barren unbecoming one;
And He cried all winter long.

And then, a fragile pink and yellow carpet
Crept from between the grains of sand;
Proud, pure white yucca candelabra rejoiced;
Bushes flamed unashamedly;
Blooms of the spectrum popped out
From fat little porcupine cacti;
Beavertails pinned on blossoms;
The Cereus flowered for the moths at night.
Each one waited its turn to live.

Ω

TURN LEFT AT ALBUQUERQUE

So mid-life surprised you, jumped up,
And shouted in your ear:
Hurry up, the rumor's out that
Time will soon disappear.
To wend your way to wisdom,
You must pick the path you like;
Pull the shade on mirages,
Put your finger in the dike;
Shovel all the doubtful 'shoulds'
Beneath the shifting sands;
Plant your feet on the bedrocks
Known as 'wants', 'dos' and 'cans'.
Look inside, there's the devil
Who won't let you do it,
Beside him is an angel
Who is whispering, "Pursue it!"
If you can take command very soon,
Life will be <u>your</u> slave,
For tombstones are just pebbles
Till they sit upon your grave.

You want to know what's wrong with you,
My loveable wild turkey:
You forgot to turn left
When you got to Albuquerque.

Ω

www.ingramcontent.com/pod-product-compliance
Lightning Source LLC
Chambersburg PA
CBHW072035060426
42449CB00010BA/2270